WORDS BY MYSELF

Anacaona Lopez

Introduction:

Welcome to a book of compilations of thoughts sporadically written since 2009. It started in college, jotting down thoughts that came to mind. Compilations of thoughts and emotions both mine and of others, observations of life; welcome to a glimpse of my story.

I'd like to thank friends, family, and past lovers for being the inspiration to the short writings in this books; guiding the emotions to write on what I've experienced as well as their experiences.

<u>HER STORIES:</u>

- **REGRETS**
- **UNTITLED**
- **PROVE**
- **THE COMPLICATIONS OF ME**
- **REALITY CHECK**
- **TIME**
- **FACING REALITY- MOVING ON**
- **COUNTING**
- **TOMORROW**
- **LOVE**
- **CURSED**
- **THE PAST**
- **ME**
- **MISTAKES**
- **FOREVER ALONE**
- **AGING**
- **A FOOL**
- **BATTLES**
- **LOVE STORIES**
- **FRIENDZONE**
- **IT COULD'VE BEEN YOU**
- **ARE YOU HERE FOR A REASON, A SEASON? MAYBE A LIFETIME?**
- **LOVE STORIES CONT.**
- **PRESSURES**
- **RIDING YOU**
- **LUST STORIES**
- **REALIZATIONS OF LIFE**
- **A MOTHER DOES**
- **DISAPPOINTMENTS**
- **FREEDOM**
- **DICK CHALLENGE (IG TREND)**
- **THOUGHTS**
- **LOVE IN THE MODERN WORLD**
- **LUST STORIES PT II**
- **TRIPPIN**
- **TEMPTATIONS**
- **ANACAONA**
- **THE KIND OF LOVE I WANT**
- **TODAY IS THE DAY**
- **THE OTHER WOMAN**
- **A WOMAN**
- **ONION**
- **SEXUALIZED**

REGRETS

Sometimes you don't realize what you had until it's gone.
It's then you realize that you had it all along,
OR maybe you were confused and thought you needed
something else.
To THEN realize you were wrong.
NOW the real question is, what's going to happen after the
mistake?
you can't just reverse life and take back what's gone.
Now you hope and wonder can this be undone, and the
person you dissed has not moved on.
Some people believe in second chances, but life is like the
wind.
You don't really know where it's coming from or when it's
going to hit you, it destroys
BUT yet makes you feel good
AND just like your mistakes you can't retrace it.

Est. August 2009

UNTITLED

I love the way you move,
how you make me laugh,
but the conversations that we barely have.
I would have never thought to feel the way I feel when I'm
with you,
sadly to say I wish it would have never went through.
before...
it was fake,
it was depressing,
I was confused,
I was ashamed,
I didn't have much to say,
I used to wonder what it was all about.
Why people make a big deal and obsess over this doubt,
that I had...
To think I used to lie,
wondering if I'll ever feel,
now that it seems so real,
I don't know what to do.
The words that are coming out my mouth are in reality true.
Before I wouldn't care what ran through your mind,
Now the thoughts race thru mine.
Hoping that you actually believe what I say and not think
that it's just another day,
or shall I say another dude that I just so happen to do.
I hate how you got me sitting here,
waiting and pondering,
I'm so pissed that it's you,
I just don't think you're worth it

Est. Sept 2009

PROVE

I give up, no matter what I say or do, I always seem to lose.
I try to make it up but it's never enough,
I'm always tryna prove, like I got something to lose.
Gotta be perfect, gotta show, because for some reason it's in season to please others
and not YOURSELF!
Why do we try so hard???
Like we aren't enough,
so we change our ways, or watch what we say,
to avoid the lost,
or to try to prove,
I give up!
No matter how hard I try, I can never seem to find the right ways
Then YOU wonder, are YOU wasting your time?
tryna impress,
but that person doesn't really care,
or is busy following someone else.
Playing the same game and it's a shame, how we string people along
Have them doubt, wonder, change, or prove that they are right for you,
like your some sort of king, sitting on a throne, making the decisions.
Whether this position is right for you, like an interview.
But I'm tired,
nobody's perfect,
we shouldn't have to prove.
People come and go, if you really look at it,
life is like a hoe.

Est. Sept 2009

THE COMPLICATIONS OF ME

As I sit in my car waiting for class, I start to write in my notepad. A lil boredom causes me to write and sometimes think, so here's a lil writing for thee

Can't say I am an open person because I'm not,
You will never really know me even though you think you've reached the top.
You may solve me like a riddle, but the pieces to the puzzle will always fumble
You think you got it?
Know my flaws?
You must have forgotten that I have my TALL walls.
There's more to me than what it seems,
Growing up in my shell for protection, from any possible rejection.
You can try to figure me out, but I highly DOUBT.

Est. October 2009

REALITY CHECK

Reality check.
You thought you were in,
But was never at the door.
It's crazy how you bring down walls; stretch out a hand,
sometimes an arm,
just to get that person.
Times when you thought, he'd call to say come over and
hang, never happened
Mothafucka slackin!
But then you receive these messages, wanting to know what
you're doing,
Where you at?
Let's hang!
That's how you know that persons real,
You realize you need to stop wasting your time with the
other because this ones the deal.
My cards are set, it's just a matter of doing something 'bout
this reality check.

Est. November 2009

TIME

Do we really have all the TIME?
Why do we put things off for tomorrow?
Or
We say we have all the TIME in the world.
Little sayings like these have you sitting at 50 wondering
where the fuck TIME went.
How you just said don't worry there's TIME,
days, weeks, months go by.
Then when it's too late, you start wondering WHY!!

Est. December 2009

FACING REALITY – MOVING ON

Some people don't get the point,
kinda like smoking a joint.
Hittin' that shit never wanting to pass,
You don't realize that no matter how much you try you're
not getting any ass.
Looking stupid thinking you'll get it one day.
Honestly, you should start stirring away.
Being persistent and consistent does not always work out.
It takes a while for some to figure it out.
Some go thru pain and never gain, hopes shot down, but as
people say life moves on.
It's only a matter of time before you realize that you were
better without.

Est. January 2010

COUNTING

I'm just counting the days, 'til I'm done.
Plucking out the pedals one by one.
This excitement that feels me up succumbs to any negative
thoughts.
Feelings that bring me down, that make me cry, weep or
doubt.
Once the days are over it'll be a chapter in my life
completed.
Ready for anything that's coming, cuz after this is over
NEVER will I feel DEFEATED

Est. February 2010

TOMORROW

People plan and save for the day to come.
Miss out on opportunities just becuz.
Take people for granted cuz they'll always be there.
But that's not guaranteed as for tomorrow may NOT be.

Est. February 2010

LOVE

Do you believe in LOVE?
Not loving someone but INLOVE?
This feeling not many can say they've encountered,
as many do confuse the matter.
When do you know it's right?
How do you know if the person you think, is the one?
Could you be wrong, and without you noticing let your
soulmate pass along?
Be stringed along by the person you think is the one for you
The real question is:
**Is it real, and possible to feel, and be right about the
person we think is meant to be in our life?**

Est. February 2010

CURSED

Ever feel like you've been cursed?
No matter how many times you try, things just end up
worse?
Always getting the same results from different people
around the world
It kinda makes you think, like WTF is going on?
What am I doing wrong??!
That no matter how many times you try or test things out,
You end up with the same run around

Est. February 2010

THE PAST

Your past is your past and there's no future in it.

So why try to relive something that past?

The clocks moving forward not back
In order to advance you must let go
Why try to retain something that was ages ago?
In order to progress you must let go of your past.

You will never progress, or ever reach success.

Remember never let your past dictate who you are, but let it
be a part of who you will become.
If you're still living in the past, you will always end up at
SQUARE ONE!

Est. May 2010

ME

I've been thru a lot since I was young but no one knows
These things I've kept bottled up, has made an impact on
today's whereabouts
I don't do it on purpose, it's not like I planned but due to
circumstances, I am where I stand.
Despite the disappointments, awkwardness, and
uncomfortable situations I've experienced,
it helped me make me, something that can never be
duplicated.

Est. July 2010

MISTAKES

The mistakes people make sometimes make them wish they
could retrace.
Turn back the hands of time and think before they make, that
DIAL.
Not everyone is perfect and errors made on their turf can
cause changes and hurt.
But that's part of life,
To live and learn,
Whether the other person wants to give you another turn I
guess you sit and wait,
Or move and then they'll be the ones to make another
mistake

                                                    Est. May 2011

FOREVER ALONE

FOREVER ALONE, seems to be the norm.
Single ladies, waiting to be picked up by their feet
give their hearts to the one they think will keep
IT.
But in return comes the lies, the deceptions, the games, our
generation has created.
Making women lose hope in relations, with the right man.
When will he come?
See don't judge a book by its cover.
Your perception is nothing but a misconception of a single
woman's life.
Once she's wife'd, she gives you all of her with all her
might.
This cycle can also represent a man's situation, but in this
day and age,
it's the women that are often hurt by the separation.
*She gave her all, thinking I've finally found the one, to be
done in the long run.*

Est. May 2014

AGING

Aging: The process of growing old
Aging, the expectations of others change
Aging, oh I got time
Aging, little to no mistaken to be done
Aging, little to no fucks given
Aging, dating is a game
Aging, where are your kids?
Aging, I can do bad all by myself
Aging, now I'm sad because I have no one else
Aging, I can travel the world
Aging, I should have the money and be on my own
Aging, why are you living with your moms?
Aging, why haven't you found the one?
Aging, is an ending process
Aging, that stops when you're no longer living

Est. May 2014

A FOOL

A fool,
Someone who is blinded and had been warned but refused to
see the truth,
they're so damn closed minded.
A fool,
Someone who sees the wrongs but hopes that this change
will come along.
A fool,
Someone who thinks they can make change; change a
persons' ways, and be their main.
A fool,
Someone who is desperate for love, settling for the affection
and attention
Not knowing that their setting themselves to get into a
depression
That ;ater leads to resentment.
A fool
Wanting to be happy and ignoring the signs, without
realizing that not everyone is like you,
Your one-of-a-kind.
A fool,
An innocent soul who only wants they deserve
Expects that another do the same, but in returned gets
CURVED

Est. May 2015

BATTLES

Dating, it's not the same anymore
The older you become the harder it is to find
Then there's you
I no longer have you, do I need you?
I've been told I don't, with age it won't matter anymore
I want to feel that it's true
That without you, my womanhood is intact like glue
But see I've become insecure
Because I don't have you
I can do bad all by myself, without YOU
Conquer the world, marry and be happy
But my heart is so pure and afraid to give in
To be hurt and cheated, to be used, because
I'm a fool
A fool for love, and to be loved is every woman's dream
Along with breeding
Something I can no longer do because I don't have you

Est. July 2015

LOVE STORIES

1. Wrap your arms around me tight
let your breath succumb my might
the swift and subtle breath I breathe of you
flows within my pores and makes me want you more.
Let me sleep tight, on the bedside
Bodies as one, until it's daylight

2. Can you be mine
I'll be yours
Lets' evolve ourselves in one
Only until tomorrow
Lets forget our sorrows

3. Feeling ALIVE is when you pull through on the
things you love to do
Compromise here and there, not giving a fuck who
cares.

4. Take me away and put aside our minds
Let our souls take the wheel to this new life
Responsibilities forgotten
Ex-lovers abandoned
Wouldn't it be so cool?
Where life could be just me and you

5. Kiss me, Bite me, Lick Me
Push Me, Shove Me, Do Me
As you please ME

6. Be free
Be you
Be her
Be new
See her
Do you
No worries…
It's everyone's story

7. I miss you
But not really you
I miss me feeling this sweet sense of being
Being in a man's arm
I'm not obsessed, I'm under stress
I need to feel comfort, feel support, by YOU
But that doesn't necessary mean I want you

8. I don't want you
I want your soul
I want all of you
Even the areas you don't know

9. Subtle taste
Drips down your waist
How sweet and tender
Is all I remember

Est. October 2016

FRIENDZONE

Friendzone
Imma put you in the friendzone
I like you but not enough
See I'm feeling myself and somebody else.
But you're cool, to KEEP right THERE
As a just in CASE, I make a mistake
So sweet of you to wait.
I'm not the type of woman to take any bait
But now, things have changed,
I sit here and think I failed in the game.
Falling for the wrong dudes,
Overlooking the right, thinking I got time, it's light.
Seeing how much you've grown, how could I have been so cold.
Making dumb decisions, crying and weeping for the man who's dreamy.
Overlooking the sweet, wondering "could you have been my king?"
Standing like a lonely soldier in war.
It's a life lesson, a closed door, I caused, nothing to do.
But now live in the friendzone like you.

Est. October 2016

IT COULD'VE BEEN YOU

It could've been you
As a matter of fact it would've been you
You shouldn't have stopped pursuing
Helped me open my eyes, to refrain me from using my
energy on somebody else.
I was just fooling myself.
The imagery of life and expectations all shattered,
Like my feelings didn't matter.
Now I sit back and think, DAMNNNN what was I drinking?
What did he give me, that I was so taken, by this drug called
LOVE
Love that went to the wrong places, and now I'm sitting here
facing,
Life with an individual who doesn't deserve my time.
A part of me could have been yours and now that's
GOODBYE.
It lingers through my mind ever so often,
It could've been you,
It should've been you.

Est. October 2016

ARE YOU HERE FOR A REASON, OR FOR A SEASON? MAYBE A LIFETIME?

Hard times come and go, what does that tell me of you?
Give me a reason to make you my muse
Physically, emotionally, spiritually I've been broken down
Come scoop me up from the ground
Fill me with your energy that I lack, before you take a hike
and never come back

Seasons, change how amazing it feels
Nature at it's best even when I'm not prepared for the glory
of nature's mess
Experiencing the variety of the earth's power, peace, make
me laugh, but not for long
Oh what a great joy to grow and share this beautiful world
with you
Hold and enjoy you tight never leave my sight
Uh Oh the weather's changing, and your off on a life's flight

Lifetime relationships teach us lifetime lessons
The buildup, the makeup, the mini break-up
Build the foundation
Let's not give up the fight, accept and love that person
regardless if you are right

So to conclude this message, are you my reason, here for a
season, or down for life?

Est. November 2016

LOVE STORIES CONT.

1. I struggle with me
I struggle with you
You're no good for me
I'm such a buffoon

2. Why can't I let you go?
You've taken my soul
This pact I indirectly bargained for
Now I live in regrets, soulless, with no shoulder to lean on

3. How should I tell you that he doesn't love you
His actions, his games, it's driving you insane
Love empowers, it does not devour
Let that shit go, your pride is slowly losing its soul

4. Girl please stop!
I'm tired of your stories
Giving you advice but you choose to ignore
The words I'm telling you, you look like a damn fool
Una mardita penka ese bicho no vale, mujer dale!
You come to me all the time, yet make no changes
My words are a lost cause, I'm honestly done with all your
phases
I love you girl, but you gotta work on you
Save the stories for someone else, I need to be by myself
Shit, got my own issues to deal with, I'm no longer
interested

Est. November 2016

PRESSURES

Pressures of life
Pressures of men
Pressures of society
Pressures of women
We all want to show off to someone
Whether it be your lover, mother, boss, best friend or
enemy
This drive forces us to live FAKE lives
WHY?

Est. January 2017

RIDING YOU

The fear and excitement when I see you I can't explain
I fear when I sit down, but my body fills with power while I
ride you,
The adrenaline that rushes through my body, through my
veins
The thoughts that run through my brain
As I continuously ride you
Looking like a PRO, having people know or shall I say
ASSUME
That I can easily handle you
Very sexy they say, you're a badass chica
Mamasita, let me get your number
Ride me like you ride this
Another level I've become, while I sit on your seat,
Owning the streets as I run,
Riding you feeling the pump in my veins
Gaining the strength and losing the fear each day

Est. September 2017

LUST STORIES

1.   We search and cannot find
We want, yet struggle to combine, the things we truly
need for our future
Lost in today's world of sex & excuses
Using our bodies to get what we want
When it's thru our minds & souls
We can truly reach our goals

2.   Love Destroys
Love Enjoys
Love Surrenders
The sex so tender

3.   He comes from a foreign place
The way he grabs my waist
Makes my every move feel like a miracle
This lust inside of me, thought it was gone, it fell asleep
He's awaken the demon's inside of me

4.   "I miss you" he says
"I want you" he says
"Let me in you" he hopes
That's no longer enough, so I won't

Est. September 2017

REALIZATIONS OF LIFE

1.   If you do what you fear the most
There's nothing that can come close to:
Tearing you down
Wearing you down
Live stress free because you took the liberty to succeed
In life, fears, and obstacles
At this point there's nothing stopping you

2. She's so fly
I sometimes wonder why,
Why she single?
Why she with me?
Is she crazy?
How many of me are out there?
Can I compare to those that may want her too?
Do I have anything to lose, if I play the dating games?
Will I get caught?
Fuck it, it's her loss
But damn she's so fly, I need to be her guy

3.   Sometimes you must humble yourself
In order to grow and be understood
Many hypocrites out there
Swearing that you're this, you're that
Never realizing that you're exactly the opposite

4.   Even a lost soul
Needs help in achieving their goals

Est. September 2017

A MOTHER DOES

You don't love your son
Act like a mother
Instead of smothering your idiotic thoughts in my head
Take a seat and listen to what I have to say
Who are you to define what a mother should do?
We aren't all alike; you should know that's true
What I perceive to be the needs to my young child
Obviously differs from yours
So sit yo'ass down on the fucking floor.
Only one person in this world carries an opinion
Not you or God, despite his Holy Spirit
It is my child who has the right to complain and say YOU
LACKED
He's the only one that fucking matters, so RELAX
And live life, caring about your well-being
Now I do recognize you mean well
But at the end of the day, I am my own person
Will do as I say, when I say, and care for myself and my
seed
As I perceive it to be

Est. September 2017

DISAPPOINTMENTS

Disappointments stem from expectations
Expectations imposed by friends, family, self
If you don't expect, nonetheless will you regret

Est. October 2017

FREEDOM

Freedom is what I ask and what I want
Let me not return back as I can't stand
Can't stand the lock up, room full of cocks
I learned my lesson and never wish to go back to that
That in which I was confined behind bars
Losing out on life

Est. October 2017

DICK CHALLENGE
(IG Trend)

What am I doing for that dick
He ain't even worth it he's got a bitch
Fucks you and her all the time
Invites another broad for extra fun
Do anything for that DICK
Side-chick my way for that dick
Lick a clit for that dick
Take it up the ass for that dick
Keep this *situationship* a secret for that dick
Oh is that your girl let me hush for that dick
Just like a pic n not comment for that dick

Est October 2017

THOUGHTS...

1. If I were locked up today would you wait and stay?
   With me….

2. Her breathe is your fresh air
   As I slowly die off your carbon dioxide
   Est. November 2017

LOVE IN THE MODERN WORLD

We live in a generation where no one talks
We live in a generation where everyone flaunts
We live in a generation where people fake
Fake lives, fake love, fake friends, fake jewelry
Where are the men that opened doors?
Where are the men that greeted you with courteous
behaviors?
Politeness, graciousness, patience
Men are too lazy or lack the soul to demonstrate he is a
gentleman.
Social media is to blame along with many other things.
Women sometimes are in the wrong.
As many use their body to achieve their goals
Lack the patience to make a man wait but that is because she
is afraid
Meanwhile others are truly in for just the fucking
But deep down is looking for loving

Est. November 2017

LUST STORIES PT II.

1. Is it wrong for me to want you to want me and
    ONLY Me?

2. When will I find my Prince charming
    Sweep me, fill me
    Not only with love but with right doings

3. I lack the patience
    Yet suffer the pain of knowing what you want from me

4. Last night you were deep inside me
    Deep within my walls
    You took my soul
    Soft strokes as I moaned your name
    Heavy breaths, love feeling endlessly amazing

5. There was something about the way…He grabbed
    me and kissed me

Est November 2017

TRIPPIN

I've given you the best of me,
Why does she get the best of you?

Est. December 2017

TEMPTATIONS

Running the streets, being the man I need to be
Learned my lesson, through the years of facing the
consequences of my actions
Left alone, confined, forced to do things I didn't want to do
Dirty cells, pissed up floors, many fights was the life
I lost you, lost my sight.
Now I'm starting off new, yet there are certain things I
continue to fight today,
Everyday.

Est. December 2017

ANACAONA

Known for her beauty, livelihood and guidance
Valiance and strong presence was one of the many features
Of her
Such a beautiful golden flower –
Anacaona
Sustenance, leadership, valiance, her existence demanded
attention
In the battles of life
Shines
A beautiful golden flower,
Carnations, dahlia, and marigolds
On the gloomiest days, by no accident was she named -
Anacaona

Est. December 2017

THE KIND OF LOVE I WANT

I want someone to go on baecations with, wake up every
morning have sex with
Someone who I'd rather spend all my weekends,
An individual that is appreciative of the things I do for him,
Appreciative of the type of woman that I am,
Thinks of me and parades me on his IG
Listens carefully and remembers the conversations we have
Then surprises me with plans, activities or we discussed that
I had with him
He doesn't take my love and soul for granted
Someone who is patient because of my confusing ways
Knows that I am the way that I am and is not seeking to
change me
Relieves my stress, by helping me rest
Someone that in his arms I feel safe and warm
To come home to and cook meals to all night long
Watch sitcoms while we cuddle
Someone my son can grow & learn from to be the man that
makes a woman as happy as his mom
A person that puts a smile and makes me dance every day,
laugh and live
Someone worth being a homebody, couch potato it up
A person who only wants to fuck me and no one else
Make love, cuddle repeat…
A person who cares about my feelings
Someone who isn't perfect but understands his flaws
Makes all effort to treat me like a queen
In return it'll be my duty to make him my king

Est. January 2018

TODAY IS THE DAY

Today is the day I'll ignore you and move on
I have to remind myself what I really want.
This isn't it, what am I doing?
What have I become?
My body is in lust
In lust over you, all I do is think about you.
I know you don't feel the same
Sometimes I read our moments as an ultimate connection
As if there was nothing in this world
The depths of our bodies intertwined as one
Loving each other physically, spiritually
My body gravitates towards you all the time
And when I sleep next to you I feel like you're mine
But you aren't, and oh how I wish I could be wrong
As much as I sense I have captured you as a whole
Reality HITS!
You praise and dwell for another bitch
While I dwell on you
How did I get caught up in this wrong?

Est. January 2018

THE OTHER WOMAN

1. While you're busy giving him the world
He's off doing the same to someone else

2. I could do all the things in the world
You'd still choose her

3.   It took some time to come to realize
I couldn't fathom being without you
Was afraid to lose you
Your efforts never really showed the same affection
I know why because she had all your attention

4.   Every day I chose to ignore the things that bothered
me
Telling you didn't change a thing
Somehow I couldn't let you go
I was cursed to be your slave
My body needed your fix
The heat
I just couldn't beat myself,
out of this toxic relationship

Est. May 2018

ONION

You peeled each layer slowly
Shedding its many layers, revealing my inner core
Broke me down, made me weak
Only to leave me hanging dry out the front door

Est. May 2018

A WOMAN

She understood him very clear but he could scarcely gage
the reality of her
Every man loves a laid-back chick, one to laugh with
One who comprehends, who doesn't argue,
Shit a best friend.
Someone who you can roll your soul and be lost to
But don't forget your chick is not a NIGGA
Not your BOY, so don't lose sight of the fact she is a
WOMAN
Has needs and wants that a man lacks full comprehension
of
Spoils and wants to be spoiled,
Loves surprises, and wants to be catered as she caters to
him
Wants to feel like he's gone above and beyond to keep her
in his life
That there is no doubt another woman has made him lose
his sight – of her
Just a few things, take notes
The rest you gotta learn.

Est. May 2018

SEXUALIZED

She wanted to be loved, not to be sexualized.
But ohhhh how that feeling of moving your body swaying to
the beats of life
Capture that on Instagram, sexify
The likes, comments, it filled
Quenched her thirst of attention
immediate, love, lusts, wants, all the world's desire.
Convinced that she only displays this for attention but lets'
not mention
deep down she's a different girl
Disney character in this cold world
Change who I am, change the sea for the sand just to stand
with someone,
What would I give if I could live, what would she pay to
spend a day warm on the
sand?
Wanting a happily ever after.
Realizing it's all fake and the mistakes of how she portrayed
herself,
Is why she sits today dwelling life.
it took observing friends like such, troubled soul.
lusting for love, yet reflecting nothing but sexual behaviors
displaying, twerking, dancing, in such ways that
immediately sex comes to mind
oh my
in the eyes of the guy, that she doesn't want to be sexualized
Giving into sexual pleasure without realizing shutting the
door closed, to be emotionally
attached, with him.
He will never see her more than what's exposed to the world
Babygirl you don't see that your exterior is defining who
you truly are inside?

Though you say you aren't, no one's going to believe that this sleeze
actually believes to be wife'd, one day.
Living depressed, repeating same cycles
wondering why the fuck no one loves HER.
Take away my body and lusty thoughts
admire, appreciate, desire me intellectually, spiritually, mentally,
NOT SEXUALLY.
Is it wrong to be desired above and beyond the bedroom sheets?
yes she sees
All her life enabling sexualized behaviors
now 30 years later, she feels disabled.
Unable to be understood, wanting that immediate lust love attention
but now realizing that it's only going to worsen chances.
Marriage, family, wifey goals
shattered every time there's a new half-naked post.

Est. November 2018

Conclude

I hope you enjoyed the short reads and were able to relate to some. Please share my writings and if posted on social media do not forget to use the following hashtags

#wordsbymyself
#wordsbymyselfbyanacaona
#wordsbymyselfbyanacaonalopez

Made in the
USA
Middletown, DE